Aussie-Flat 20 Milestone Challenges: Naughty & Nice

Aussie-Flat Milestones for Memorable Moments, Grooming, Care, Socialization, Training

Volume 1

Todays Doggy

Copyright © 2023

All rights reserved. Without limiting rights under the copyright reserved above, no part of this publication may be reproduced, stored, introduced into a retrieval system, distributed or transmitted in any form or by any means, including without limitation photocopying, recording, or other electronic or mechanical methods, without the prior written permission of the publisher, except in the case of brief quotations embodied in critical reviews and certain other non-commercial uses permitted by copyright law.

The scanning, uploading, and/or distribution of this document via the internet or via any other means without the permission of the publisher is illegal and is punishable by law. Please purchase only authorized editions and do not participate in or encourage electronic piracy of copyrightable materials

Dedicated To All of You Wonderful Owners and Fans

Introduction

Welcome to the Original Doggy Milestone Series™ where you are encouraged to create those special moments with your pup. We have composed the milestones in a way that challenges you to set the stage before taking your photos.

Use props and make it fun - be creative in setting up your photos. Get family and friends involved - take it out with you - use it in different places and settings - have a play with it and most importantly, have a good time!

Good luck and enjoy your photo fun.

Across The Floor

I
Just
Sniffed

A Dog's Bum

Last Night I Ate 2 String Bits…

Today They Came Out Tied Together

I S#*t You KNOT!

Good Morning

There's a chance I Just Pooed Over There

I Love Chewing On Everything

...Even If It's Not Mine

I
Like
Big
Mutts

and I Can Not Lie

You're Barking Up The Wrong Tree

I Don't Know Where Your Slippers Are

Whilst You Were Out...

I Did a Naughty Thing

I'm Off To Hide Now

Oooh I Smell

I NEED A DEEP CLEAN

I Was Hungry

So I Tried Feeding Myself

I Jump On Everyone I see

Without Asking Them

Yup I Just Wee'd

On The Floor

I Ate a Gross Thing Today

Not Looking Forward To Pooping It Out

Haven't Seen The Post Man In a Long Time

Maybe He's Still Traumatized

Me? a Good Pup?

Oh I Knew That Already Thanks

Hijacking

The Boss' Bed

You Just Bathed Me...

and I've Made Another Mess.

Woops!

Want To Start Doggy Yoga?

Start By Bending Over To Pick Up Your S#*t!

Every Snack You Make, Every Meal You Bake,

Every Bite You Take, I'll Be Watching You

My Favorite Hobby

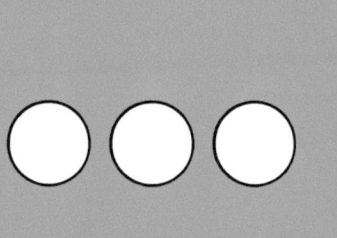

www.ingramcontent.com/pod-product-compliance
Lightning Source LLC
Chambersburg PA
CBHW041509010526
44118CB00006B/196